First published 2000 by Aurum Press Limited,
25 Bedford Avenue, London WC1B 3AT
Compilation copyright © 2000 Michelle Lovric

A catalogue record for this book is available from the British Library.

ISBN: 1-85410-736-4

Editorial assistant: Kristina Blagojevitch
Designed by Michelle Lovric and Lisa Pentreath

Printed and bound in Italy by LEGO SpA

The editor gratefully acknowledges the assistance of the following people: Judith Grant, Iain Campbell, David Franks and Lynne Curran, and the kind permission of Ronald Lockley to quote from his excellent book, *The Private Life of the Rabbit*, 1964.

ILLUSTRATION ACKNOWLEDGEMENTS:

Front cover and pages 1, 26—27, detail from La Dame à la Licorne: "Le Gout"; endpapers, detail from La Dame à la Licorne: "La Ouïe", both courtesy of the musée du Moyen-Age — Cluny, copyright © Photo RMN—R. G. Ojeda.
Page 9, detail of the Madonna with the Rabbits, Titian, Musée du Louvre, Paris, copyright © Photo RMN.
Page 3, A Young Hare in a Landscape, Heinrich Lihl; page 38, Hounds chasing Hares, Jan Van Kessell I, courtesy of Raphael Valls Ltd, London.
Page 6, The Rabbit Warren, circle of Philipe-Ferdinand de Hamilton; page 12, Decorative design, Ferdinando Albertolli; page 17, A Hare Sitting, George Stevens; page 18, Rabbits, Olaf August Hermansen; page 20, Rabbits, Horatio Henry Couldery; page 24, Rabbits, Follower of Stephen Elmer; page 37, The White Rabbit, John Roddam Spencer Stanhope, all courtesy of Sotheby's Picture Library, London.
Page 10, Ancient Greek phiale, showing a hare hunt; page 11, A Peasant Holding Two Hares, Egypt, c. 1400 BC, both copyright © The British Museum.
Victorian scraps reproduced courtesy of Mamelok Press Limited, Bury St Edmunds, England.

RABBITS

The rabbit fondles his
own harmless face ...

Alfred, Lord Tennyson (1809—92)
English poet

ontents

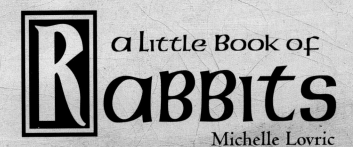

A Little Book of Rabbits

Michelle Lovric

AURUM PRESS

ntroduction

There is no creature with so diverse a range of symbolic meanings as the rabbit. Hares and rabbits have somehow come to be symbols of both sensuality and innocence, fearfulness and great feats of cunning. Rabbits are supposed to bring good luck or evil fortune, and can signify both domesticity and the call of the wild, both immortality and sudden death.

The rabbit was an ancient symbol of meekness. In his own bestiary Leonardo da Vinci observed that the rabbit is always timid, often frightened by falling leaves. In European art and writing, such gentleness has often been contrasted with the ferocity of other beasts, to make metaphorical points about human nature. The worried white rabbit of Lewis Carroll's *Alice's Adventures in Wonderland*, for example, is a deft depiction of stress and fear in a hostile world. Paradoxically, the rabbit itself has also been an object of great fear: it is thought to bring danger to fishermen and others.

Both rabbits and hares are frequently represented as cunning tricksters, able to outwit a fox or a farmer. The wise-guy rabbit, like Bugs Bunny, cultivates an air of innocence, while achieving his own ends in subtle ways. Brer Rabbit, created by Joel Chandler Harris in his *Uncle Remus* tales, is a jolly rapscallion. Sanskrit and Slavonic legends include rogue rabbits of this ilk, too. Beatrix Potter's Peter Rabbit and his friends show a milder, more appealing kind of cunning.

Both rabbits and hares, as defenceless, fearful creatures, came to be used as a symbol of those who put their hopes of safety and salvation in Christ.

For this reason, they are frequently found in paintings of the Madonna and Child. They were also symbols of lust and fertility, thus the white rabbits and hares in the religious images represented Mary's triumph over sensuality. The old belief that rabbits and hares could reproduce without mating also drew parallels with the Virgin birth.

The sexual fervour of the rabbit has been much promulgated. It is no coincidence that Hugh Hefner chose it as the symbol of his *Playboy* magazine. Many religions have associated rabbits and hares with fertility. Artemis, the ancient Greek goddess of both purity and fecundity, was often represented by rabbits. The well-known phrase "Mad as a March hare" refers to the display of manic sexual energy during the mating season. Hares were even thought to be able to change gender.

The hare and rabbit have been associated with the moon in the myths of India, China, Africa, Mexico, North America and Europe. Easter, celebrated on the first Sunday after spring's new moon, has acquired an Easter Bunny symbol, probably because rabbits have always been the first animals to breed when winter ends. Buddha is said to have appeared as a hare, who sacrificed himself to a hungry beggar. The face of a hare was thereafter to be seen imprinted on the full moon.

The hare has always been considered as a melancholy beast in Western culture. Eating his flesh was supposed to cause sadness in men. Seeing a white hare was believed to mean bad luck, as witches were said to transform themselves into hares. On the other hand, in China, rabbits were thought to be able to create the elixir of life, and the Algonquin Indians believed that their rabbit god personified the life-force. In Egyptian hieroglyphs, the rabbit symbol simply meant "to be".

The Beloved Rabbit

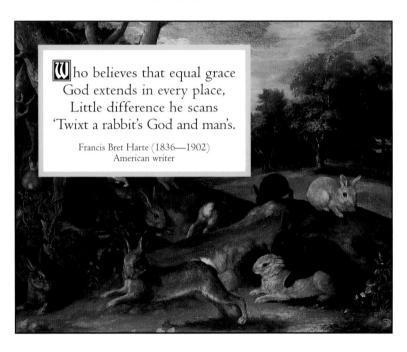

Who believes that equal grace
God extends in every place,
Little difference he scans
'Twixt a rabbit's God and man's.

Francis Bret Harte (1836—1902)
American writer

& the very human hare

The rabbit has a baby face, of rounded outlines, snub nose, enormous ears and eyes, and an appearance of helplessness ... Some students of human psychology have suggested that the preference for the round, baby-like head ... can be traced to an old deep-seated primitive instinct in man. We accept roundness because it is a feminine shape, seductive, receptive, protective ...

Ronald Lockley (b. 1903)
Welsh writer

Psychologists and behaviourists are fully aware of the appeal of the rabbit. Its popularity as a nursery toy, as a figure in childhood stories, and as a pet, are all indicative of the feelings that it arouses in a very large proportion of human beings.

Harry V. Thompson and Alastair N. Worden
from *The Rabbit*, 1956.

And as long as we ourselves possess some of the hare's apparent attributes — its unpredictableness, its occasional jumping right over the head of reason, its sharpness, its seasonal abandon, and its frequent stupidity — the myth of the hare will not be entirely dead.

George Ewart Evans and David Thomson
from *The Leaping Hare*, 1972.

THE WHITE HARE

It was the Sabbath eve: we went,
My little girl and I, intent
The twilight hour to pass,
Where we might hear the waters flow,
And scent the freighted winds that blow
Athwart the vernal grass ...

The cooling dews their balm distill'd;
A holy joy our bosoms thrill'd;
Our thoughts were free as air;
And by one impulse moved, did we
Together pour, instinctively,
Our songs of gladness there.

The green-wood waved its shade hard by,
While thus we wove our harmony:
Lured by the mystic strain,
A snow-white hare, that long had been
Peering from forth her covert green,
Came bounding o'er the plain.

Her beauty 'twas a joy to note;
The pureness of her downy coat,
Her wild, yet gentle eye;
The pleasure that, despite her fear,
Had led the timid thing so near,
To list our minstrelsy!

All motionless, with head inclined,
She stood, as if her heart divined
The impulses of ours,
Till the last note had died, and then
Turn'd half reluctantly again
Back to her green-wood bowers.

Once more the magic sounds we tried;
Again the hare was seen to glide
From out her sylvan shade;
Again, as joy had given her wings,
Fleet as a bird she forward springs
Along the dewy glade.

Go, happy thing! disport at will;
Take thy delight o'er vale and hill,
Or rest in leafy bower:
The harrier may beset thy way,
The cruel snare thy feet betray!
Enjoy thy little hour!

We know not, and we ne'er may know,
The hidden springs of joy and woe
That deep within thee lie:
The silent workings of thy heart,
They almost seem to have a part
With our humanity!

Anna Maria Wells
19th-century American poet

9

Rabbits are frequently found in pictures of the Madonna and Child ... An example is Titian's *Madonna of the Rabbit* in the Louvre. Although in a case like this, where Mary actually touches the little creature, and where, as in this picture, it is white, there may be further suggestion of the control of sensuality by the Virgin purifying the symbol, but this meaning does not replace the other; it merely adds to it.

Herbert Friedmann (1900—87)
American writer on nature and art

Rabbit Lore

Rabbits have been known from the earliest periods of history.

from Beeton's Dictionary of Natural History, 1871.

The scientific name bestowed on our little friend is *Lepus cuniculus*, and he belongs to the *Leporidae*, or hare tribe.

from *Who Were the First Miners?*, 1874.

It may be safely inferred that in early times the rabbit was not indigenous either in Greece or Italy, nor was it known eastward of these countries. The ancient Jews were unacquainted with it, and there is no mention of it in the Bible.

James Edmund Harting
from *The Rabbit*, 1898.

They tell us that he originally passed into tawny Spain from more torrid Africa, though as to whether he was introduced by the invading Arabs, swam the Straits ... the soundest historians are not agreed. Be that as it may, it seems certain that Spain is his European *Stammland*, whence he has spread over all southern countries to the shores of the Aegean.

Alexander Innes Shand (1832—1907)
Scottish journalist and writer

Rabbits in the warren,
tree in the wood.

Traditional toast

Hare horns, tortoise hairs.
(Almost impossible to find.)

Chinese proverb

With money one can
even buy rabbit-cheese.

Rumanian proverb

It's hard to put a grain
of salt on a hare's tail.

Irish proverb

RABBIT AND HARE SUPERSTITIONS

BAD LUCK
A rabbit passing behind you; killing a hare; seeing or killing
a black rabbit; dreaming of rabbits; a hare crossing the path of
a bride and groom, or of someone about to take a journey.
A pregnant woman seeing a hare: her child will have a harelip.
A hare near a ship: danger at sea for sailors.
A rabbit or a hare running down a street: a fire is imminent.

GOOD LUCK
Saying "White Rabbits" on the first day of the month.
Seeing a brown hare: you may make a wish.

RABBIT REMEDIES
Against oversleeping: eat hares' brains in wine.
Against bad behaviour in children: eat rabbit brains.
Against rheumatism: carry the left foot of a hare.
Against pleurisy: wear rabbit-skin socks.

RABBIT AND HARE DREAMS
Dreaming of rabbits: Shows a longing for protection,
but can also indicate an interest in fertility and a longing
for the countryside.
Dreaming of hares: a sign that you have enemies.

The hare, the hare-kin,
Old Big-Bum, Old Bouchart,
The hare-ling, the frisky one,
Old Turpin, the fast traveller,
The way-beater, the white-spotted one,
The lurker in ditches, the filthy beast,
Old Wimount, the coward,
The slink-away, the nibbler,
The one it's bad luck to meet, the white-livered,
The scutter, the fellow in the dew,
The grass nibbler, Old Goibert,
The one who doesn't go straight home, the traitor,
The friendless one, the cat of the wood,
The starer with wide eyes, the cat that lurks in the broom,
The purblind one, the furze-cat,
The clumsy one, the blear-eyed one,
The wall-eyed one, the looker to the side,
And also the hedge-frisker,
The stag of the stubble, long-eared,
The animal of the stubble, the springer,
The wild animal, the jumper,
The short animal, the lurker,
The swift-as-wind, the skulker,
The shagger, the squatter in the hedge,
The dew-beater, the dew-hopper,

The sitter on its form,
  the hopper in the grass,
The fidgety-footed one,
  the sitter on the ground,
The light-foot, the sitter in the bracken,
The stag of the cabbages, the cropper of herbage,
The low creeper, the sitter-still,
The small-tailed one, the one who turns to the hills,
The get-up quickly,
The one who makes you shudder,
The white-bellied one,
The one that takes refuge with the lambs,
The numbskull, the food mumbler,
The niggard, the flincher,
The one who makes people flee, the covenant-breaker,
The snuffler, the cropped head
(His chief name is Scoundrel),
The stag with the leathery hornes,
The animal that dwells in the corn,
The animal that all men scorns,
The animal that no one dare name.

Late 13th-century poem, probably from the Welsh borders. The poem was designed as
a ritual to be recited by the hunter on first encountering a hare. The 77 names were
a kind of magic spell to deliver it into his hands.

Most timid of creatures

Creatures

To rabbits, everything unknown is dangerous.

Richard Adams (b. 1920)
English novelist

The warie Hare (whose feare oft sport) hath made
Doth seek by swiftnesse death in vaine to shunne,
As if a flight of flames could be out-runne.

Sir William Alexander, Earl of Stirling (1567?—1640)
Scottish poet and statesman

The timid rabbit hails th'impervious gloom,
Eludes the dog's keen scent, and shuns her doom.

Ann Yearsley (1756—1806)
English poet

... from my path the hare
Fled like a shadow ...

Henry Wadsworth Longfellow (1807—82)
American poet

Bunny, thrilled by unknown fears,
Raised his soft and pointed ears,
Mumbled his prehensile lip,
Quivered his pulsating hip ...

Francis Bret Harte (1836—1902)
American writer

Snowy flit of a scut,
He was in his hole:
And — stamp, stamp, stamp!
... The whole world darkened
A Human near!

Walter de la Mare (1873—1956)
English poet

THE HUNTED HARE

By this, poor Wat,* far off upon a hill,
Stands on his hinder legs with listening ear,
To hearken if his foes pursue him still:
Anon their loud alarums he doth hear;
And now his grief may be compared well
To one sore sick that hears the passing-bell.

Then shalt thou see the dew-bedabbled wretch
Turn, and return, indenting with the way;
Each envious briar his weary legs doth scratch,
Each shadow makes him stop, each murmur stay:
For misery is trodden on by many,
And being low never relieved by any.

William Shakespeare (1564—1616)
English poet and playwright
* the hare

If they hear the dogs, they raise themselves on their legs and run from them; but if fearful imagination oppress them, as they oftentimes are very sad and melancholy, supposing to hear the noise of dogs where there are none such stirring, then do they run to and fro, fearing and trembling, as if they were fallen mad.

Edward Topsell (?—1638)
English religious writer

Shapes & styles of Rabbits

Man has, by the selection of individuals with desired characters of size, colour, structure ... produced an astonishing variety of "breeds" of tame rabbits: the long-woolled Angora, the hare-like (but true rabbit) Belgian Hare, the meat and fur-bearing giants — Beveren, Flemish and New Zealand breeds, the Lop-Ear with its immense trailing ears, and many others of different colours, sizes and physical peculiarities.

Ronald Lockley (b. 1903)
Welsh writer

There are four varieties of rabbits, differing somewhat in their characteristics and habits, namely, the *warreners, parkers, hedgehogs,* and *sweethearts.* The first kind, as their name implies, are in the habit of making their homes or burrows in open grounds or warrens; the *hedgehogs* are found in thick hedgerows and wood covers ... the *parkers* live on the upland also, as in gentlemen's parks, pleasure-grounds, and broad open grazing grounds ... *Sweethearts* are the tame varieties, and now multiplied into innumerable varieties of size, colour, and character, from the olden to the lop-eared, and from the middle-sized to the monster of ten pounds weight.

from *Beeton's Dictionary of Natural History,* 1871.

RABBITS ARE GENERALLY

Emilius Albert de Cossor

The rabbit, with its short legs, only half the length of a hare's, and its shorter body, twists and swerves aside with a jerky motion, and really seems to be going at a tremendous pace. The hare, with her long legs, and the stride and grace of a racehorse, moves away so evenly that most people do not realize her true speed.

James Edmund Harting
from *The Rabbit*, 1898.

22

... rabbit, fleeing with flirt and jump ...

Elizabeth Akers Allen
(1832—1911)
American poet

[Hares] are slender, graceful little creatures, with long ears, which are constantly moving, and very prominent eyes, with which they can see both before and behind.

Peter Parley (William Martin) (1801—67)
English writer

A hare will wait watching you until you are almost upon her, and then with one bound, long and high, start leaping away ... her ears erect even in flight — only when pressed at full speed are the ears laid back — her tail horizontal ... her long, thin back now arched, now lengthened, like a snake's.

George Ewart Evans and David Thomson
from *The Leaping Hare*, 1972.

23

Ah, Coney base,
Why do this harm,
With baby face
And whiskered charm!

E. L. G.

Appetites & instincts

Its little excursions to nibble carrots, lettuces, peas are tiresome, but, like the misbehaviour of children whom we nevertheless love, can be corrected by our own watchfulness. Like children, the rabbits in garden, field and hutch endear themselves to us by their innocent, happy preoccupation with their simple way of living.

Ronald Lockley (b. 1903)
Welsh writer

25

In the choice of food rabbits do not appear to be very particular. They will eat almost anything that is green.

James Edmund Harting
from *The Rabbit*, 1898.

Next to man and his domestic animals, rabbits are the prime architects of our landscape.

Harry V. Thompson
and Alastair N. Worden
from *The Rabbit*, 1956.

FROM "BRER RABBIT
AND THE TAR-BABY", 1904.

An' all de creeturs wuz in de same fix,
Ceppin' ol' Brer Rabbit,
wid his errytatin' tricks;
He went his way, an' he had his fun
Ef de branch wuz dry er ef it run;
He loped along wid his lippity-clips,
A-wigglin' his nose an' a-workin' his lips,
An' his mornin' drink wuz allers new —
It wuz sweet-gum sap an' honey-dew!

Joel Chandler Harris (1848—1908)
American writer

E'en the coy hare blest with her cheering smile
Slinks from its buried solitudes awhile
From woodland lares all winters wants could find
Where brown sedge whistled to the restless wind
To clover leas & there it squats to play
In timid raptures dewy hours away ...
Then off it scampers mid the shielding grain
Till all is still & out it skips again
& the wild rabbit less reserved & coy
Squats on the heaths thyme hills in nibbling joy ...

John Clare (1793—1864)
English poet

All things that love the sun are out of doors;
The sky rejoices in the morning's birth;
The grass is bright with rain-drops; —
   on the moors
The hare is running races in her mirth;
And with her feet she from the plashy earth
Raises a mist, that glittering in the sun,
Runs with her all the way, wherever she doth run.

William Wordsworth (1770—1850)
English poet

27

Sitting like a small opossum,
On his hind-legs raised, a rabbit
Sees a tossing clover blossom,
And essays in vain to grab it;
While an old one on his haunches,
Seeming not at all to mind him,
Peers straight at me through the branches,
With his ears erect behind him.

Hugh Haliburton (James Logie Robertson) (1846—1922)
Scottish poet

Rabbits can count up to four. Any number above four is Hrair — "a lot", or "a thousand".

Richard Adams (b. 1920)
English novelist

A hare is a curious creature:
like a child it wants to know what is going on.

George Ewart Evans and David Thomson
from *The Leaping Hare*, 1972.

Far from being childishly cute, they possessed by nature great courage and resourcefulness within, as it were, the ambit of the limits, strength, and qualities given them by the Creator.

Richard Adams (b. 1920)
English novelist

En passant, we may say that Rabbits can bite, when they are disposed, and have a favourable opportunity.

Charles Arthur House and Allan Watson
from *Rabbits and All About Them*, 1919.

They are quarrelsome and mischievous animals ...

from *The Complete Rabbit Fancier*, 1823.

Small wonder that in the traditional nursery tales the rabbit is both the *enfant terrible* and the lovable character. Beatrix Potter and a hundred other authors have created the acceptable image of careless, cheerful, clever Rabbit ... Uncle Remus's Brer Rabbit always wins in the battle of wits with Brer Fox; Baby Face triumphs once more over Long-Nose.

Ronald Lockley (b. 1903)
Welsh writer

"Didn't the fox never catch the rabbit, Uncle Remus?" asked the little boy.

Joel Chandler Harris (1848—1908)
American writer
from *Uncle Remus*, 1880.

The rabbit has a charming face;
Its private life is a disgrace.
I really dare not name to you
The awful things that rabbits do.

Anonymous

They have such lost, degraded souls,
No wonder they inhabit holes.

Anonymous

Love life & family life

"A wonderful thing to be in love," sighed the little Rabbit,
as he sat under a great fern on the hillside.

Comtesse Elen Soumarokoff-Elston
from *The Amorous Rabbit*, 1925.

The fecundity of the wild rabbit is great, and if we should calculate the produce from a single pair in one year, the number would be amazing. They will breed eleven times a year, and bring forth generally, in their wild state, eight young ones each time ... at the end of four years a couple of rabbits shall see a progeny of almost a million and a half.

from *The Complete Rabbit Fancier*, 1823.

The weariness of my heart on the hares and the young women who won't be satisfied.

Irish hare curse

RABBITS' HONEYMOONS, LIKE

Emilius Albert de Cosson,

I was born underground in the middle of May;
At least so I heard my old mother say.
Nine nice little brothers and sisters I had,
But I do not remember the face of my dad.
We were all very happy from morning till night;
We all loved to play, but never to fight.
We lived upon milk till our teeth came to chew,
Then we nibbled the turnips and carrots a few;
Oats, barley, and wheat to us were the same,
And from sweet Kitty Clover we could not refrain.

Captain M.
From *The Life and Perils of a Little Rabbit*, 1868.

THEIR LIVES, ARE SHORT.

om *Heartsease and the Rabbits*, 1882.

The Hares of olden time were wont
To lead a peaceful life:
A happier couple ne'er was seen
Than March Hare and his wife.

Arthur S. Gibson
from *The March Hares and Their Friends*, 1883.

It was said that the female hare escaped from the Ark and was drowned, and when the animals came out there was only one. So God gives him the power to bear children.

George Ewart Evans and David Thomson
from *The Leaping Hare*, 1972.

[The Hare] keepeth not her young ones together in one litter, but layeth them a furlong from one another, that so she may not lose them altogether, if peradventure men or beasts light upon them.

Edward Topsell (?—1638)
English religious writer

The Caressing Pet

The rabbit is a caressing animal,
and equally fond with the cat
of the head being stroked.

from *The Complete Rabbit Fancier*, 1823.

The poet William Cowper kept three pet hares, Puss, Tiney and Bess, as domestic pets. Puss was his favourite, and Cowper described his behaviour:

Puss grew presently familiar, and would leap into my lap, raise himself upon his hinder feet, and bite the hair from my temples. He would suffer me to take him up, and to carry him about in my arms, and has more than once fallen fast asleep on my knee.

Cowper nursed Puss through an illness, and the hare showed gratitude:
a sentiment which he most significantly expressed by licking my hand, first the back of it, then the palm, then every finger separately, then between all the fingers, as if anxious to leave no part of it unsaluted ...

William Cowper (1731—1800)
English poet

Why should I not paint the portrait of Baptiste himself, Baptiste the tame rabbit with a lion's heart? For years and years he mounted guard over his mistress, the fruitwoman in the rue de la Tour. Huge, with ears in tatters and eyes that never missed a thing, he sat in state on her doorstep, among the crates. Woe betide any passing dog! And woe to the intruder who ventured to squeeze the fruitwoman's arm or waist.

Sidonie Gabrielle Colette (1873—1954)
French novelist

THE LITTLE WHITE RABBIT

"May I go to the field," said the little white rabbit,
"Where the corn grows sweet and high?"
"Is there aught on the stile," said the old, old mother,
"Or what do I there espy?"

"'Tis a shepherd's lad, but he dreams in his place,
And he will not rise to slay."
"Oh, do not trust to an idle hand,
So stay, my little one, stay."

"There comes one now," said the little white rabbit,
"Through the corn so sweet and high."
"And so there are two," laughed the old, old mother,
"And you dare not pass them by."

"'Tis a farmer's lass, and she sings as she comes,
And she smiles upon her way."
"Is she young, is she fair, as she lilts her song?
Now say, my pretty one, say."

"She is gold as the field," said the little white rabbit,
"Where the sun all day doth lie;
She is fair as the snow is, my old, old mother,
And grey as the mist her eye."

"If the lass be fair, as you say that she be,
With her hair like the setting sun —
Oh, he never will wait to look on you,
So run, my little one, run."

Dora Sigerson (1866—1918)
English poet

Life & Death

If it were not for the extraordinary fecundity of the rabbit, the number of litters to which a doe will give birth in a year, and the number of young produced in each litter, the species *Lepus cuniculus*, with such a host of enemies, foremost of which is man, must long ago have become extinct. As if it were not enough to face the gun, and run the risk of capture by ferret, gin, brass wire, or drop-down net, the unfortunate "Bunter" has a host of natural enemies to contend with, both furred and feathered.

James Edmund Harting
from *The Rabbit*, 1898.

He dies, and rejoices to know
that so many more will take his place.

Hilaire Belloc (1870—1953)
French-born British writer

FROM "EPITAPH ON A HARE"

His frisking was at evening hours,
For then he lost his fear,
But most before approaching showers,
Or when a storm drew near.

Eight years and five round rolling moons
He thus saw steal away,
Dozing out all his idle noons,
And every night at play.

I kept him for his humour's sake,
For he would oft beguile
My heart of thoughts that made it ache,
And force me to a smile.

But now beneath his walnut shade
He finds his long last home,
And waits, in snug concealment laid,
Till gentler Puss shall come.

William Cowper (1731—1800)
English poet
Puss was one of Cowper's pet hares.

And the rabbit from his burrow
Slyly slinks along the furrow,
Where the high corn hides his route,
Looking timidly about,
Lest the poacher's lurcher nigh
Track him, with far-watchful eye,
To his haunts 'mid fragrant thyme,
And so bite him, ere his prime,
With sure teeth as tooth of Time.

Cornelius Webb (1790?—1850?)
English poet